My First Big ABC

Ages 3-5

Vol.3 G·H·I

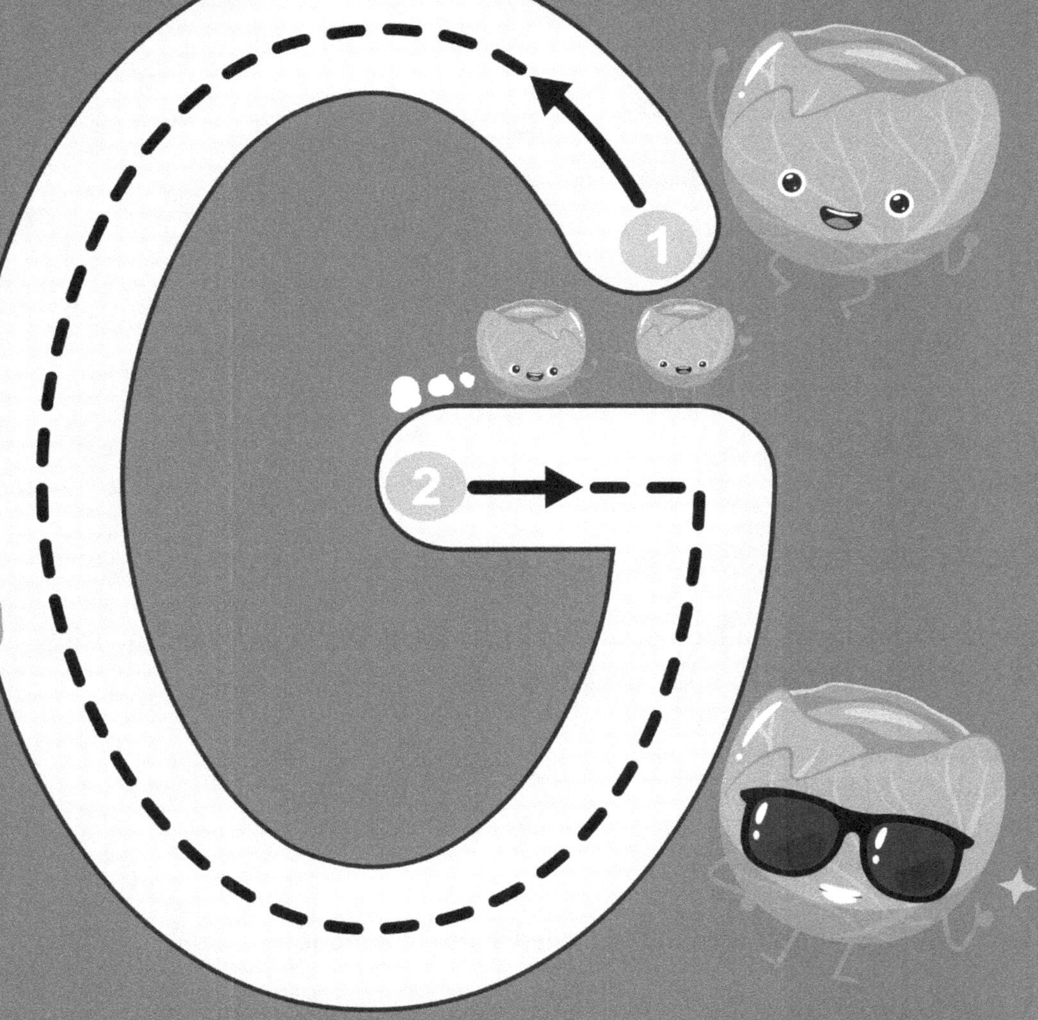

My First Big ABC Book Series
Big Sailor Edu

For permission requests, bulk order information, or any busine ss related inquries, please contact the publisher at the email address below.

Cambridge Dynasty Press
30 N Gould St. STE4000
Sheridan, WY 82801
Email: Bestsailoredu@Gmail.com

Written, Designed, and Printed in the United States of America

978-1-7357844-5-8(Paperback)

47678459

Hi! Nice to meet you.
My name is Cabbagedu!

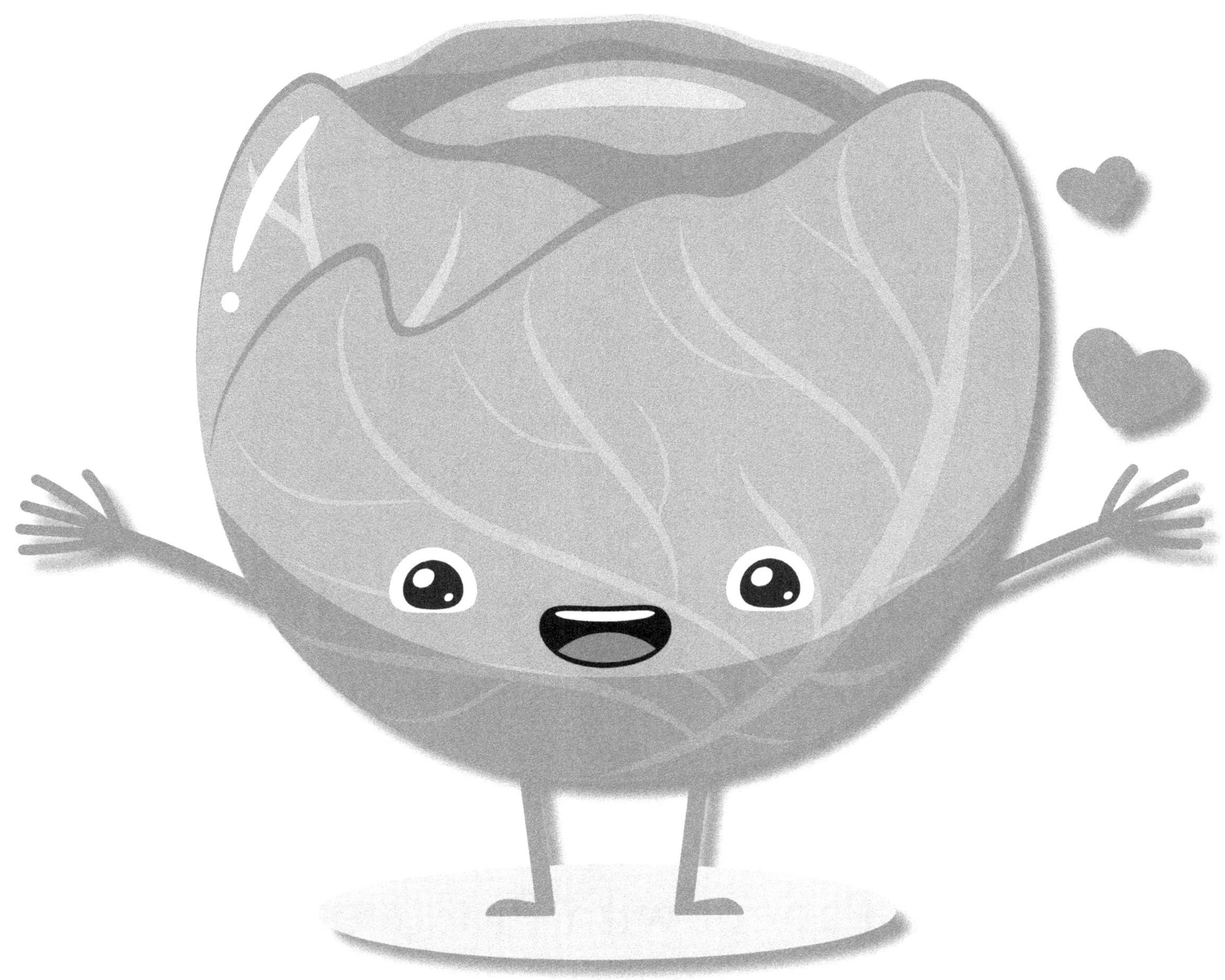

I am your study buddy
for this book!

1. Building Skills for Pen Control
2. Recognizing Alphabet Letters
3. Building Confidence
4. Enjoying a Good Book
5. Being Patient with Practice
6. Developing Creative Thinking
7. Being Proud of Achievement
8. Having Fun

This book belongs to

____

(name)

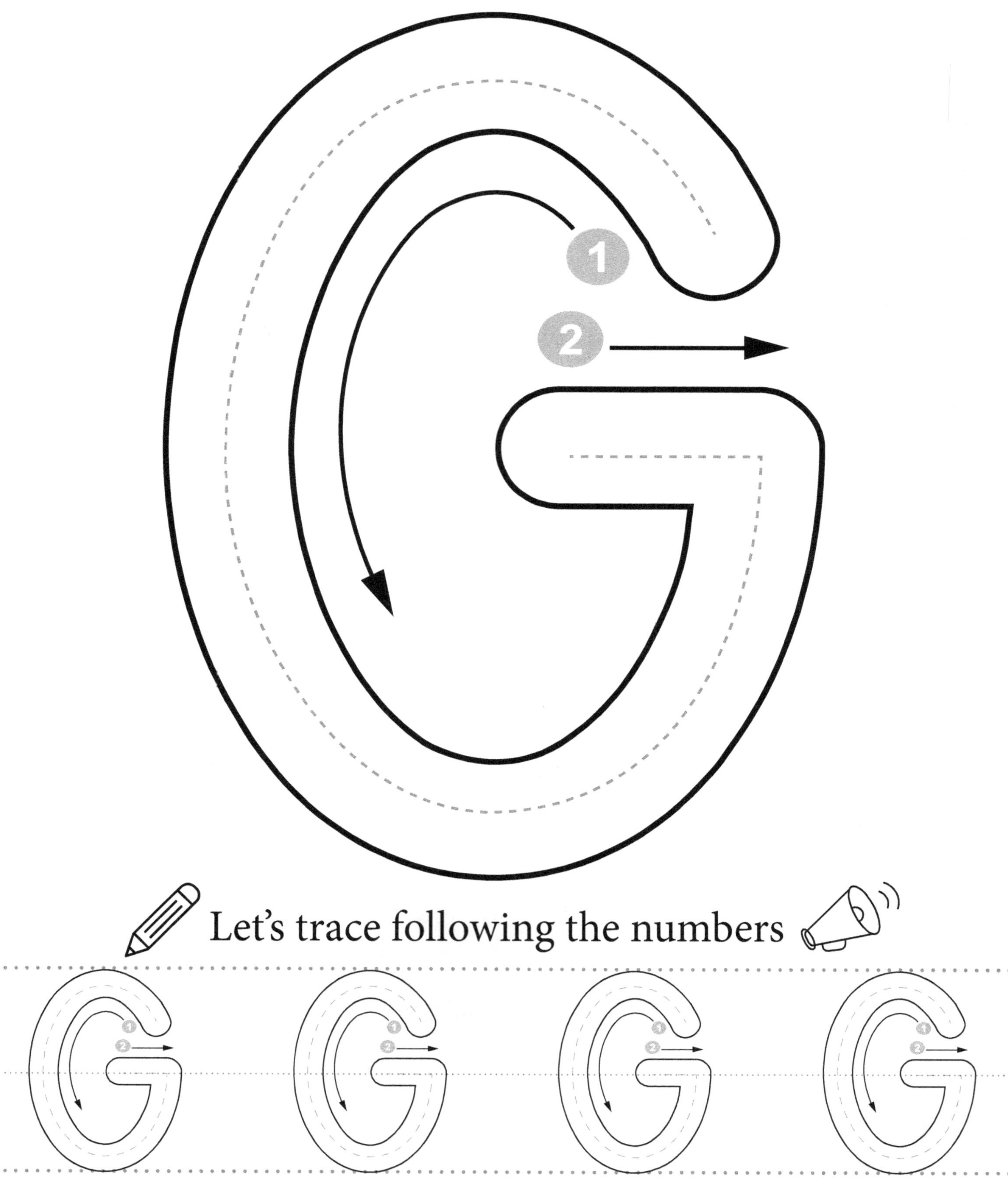

Let's trace following the numbers

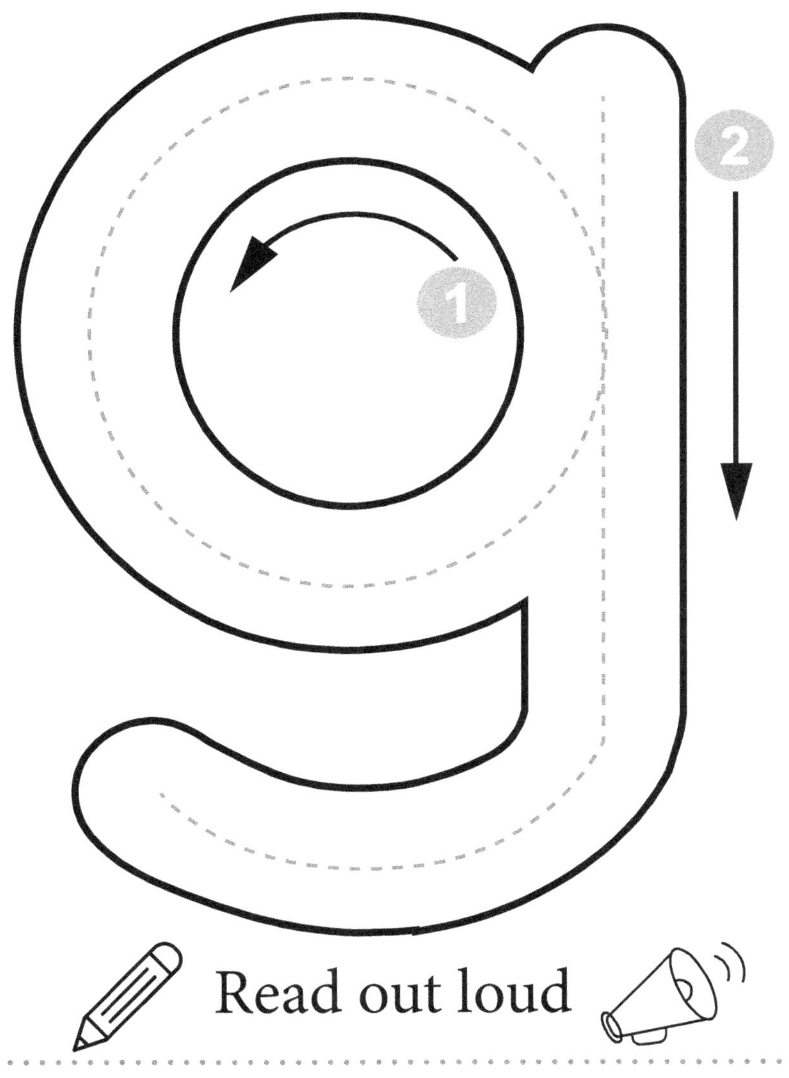

Read out loud

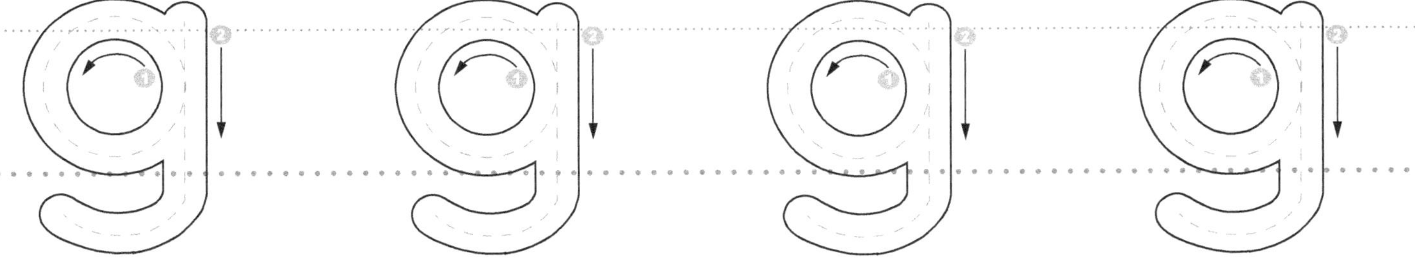

Glasses

 Let's trace following the numbers 

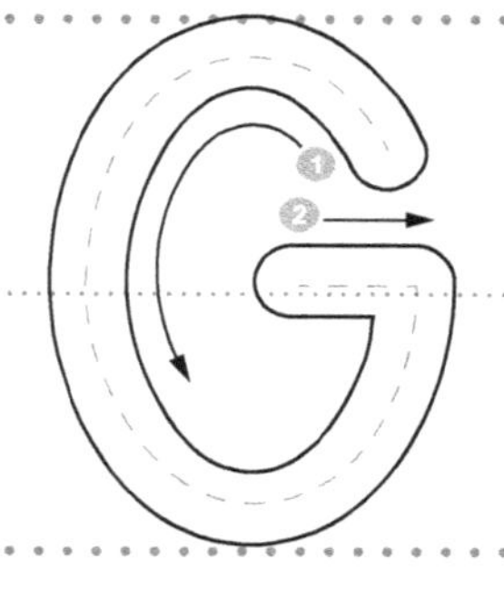 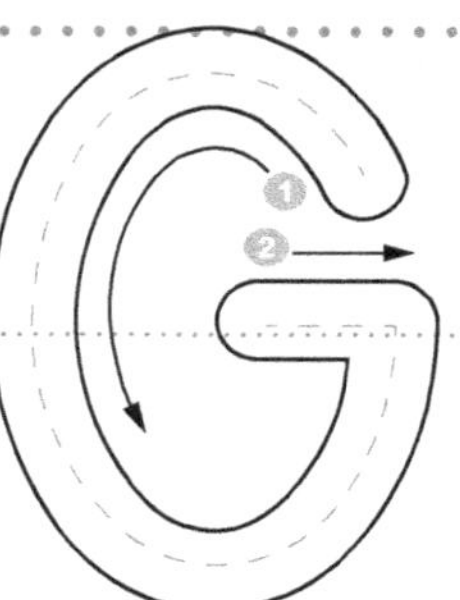 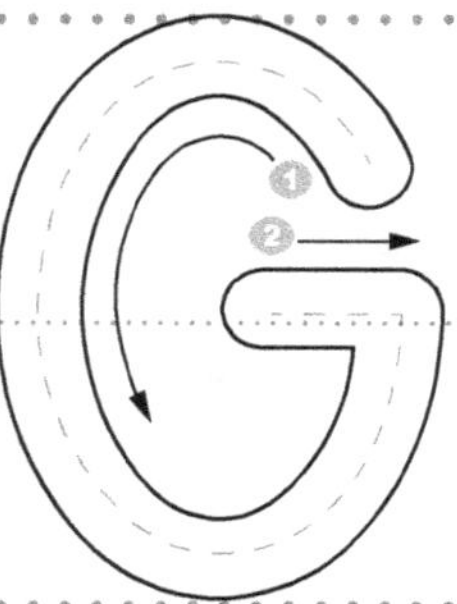 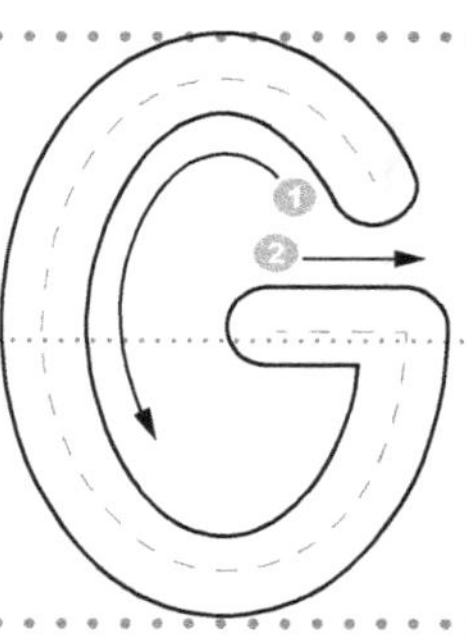

Giraffe

grape

Read out loud

 g  g   g   g

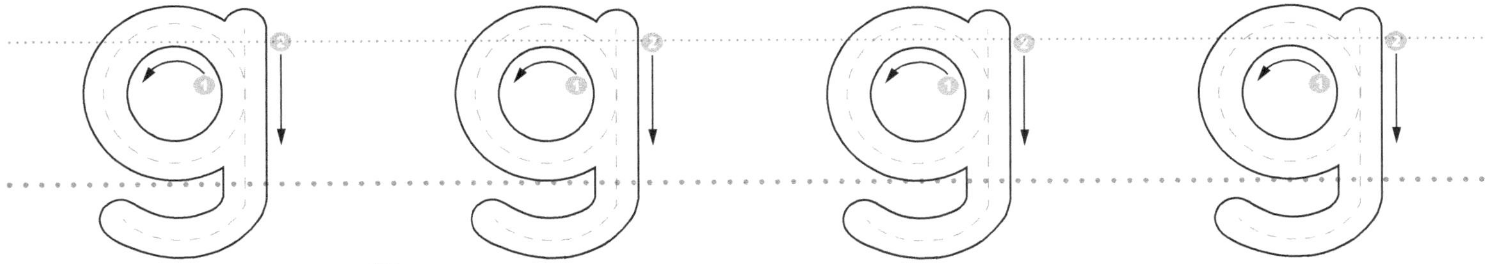

goat

Find every G and color them

10

Well done!
Let's keep
going.

Trace the dotted line and read out loud

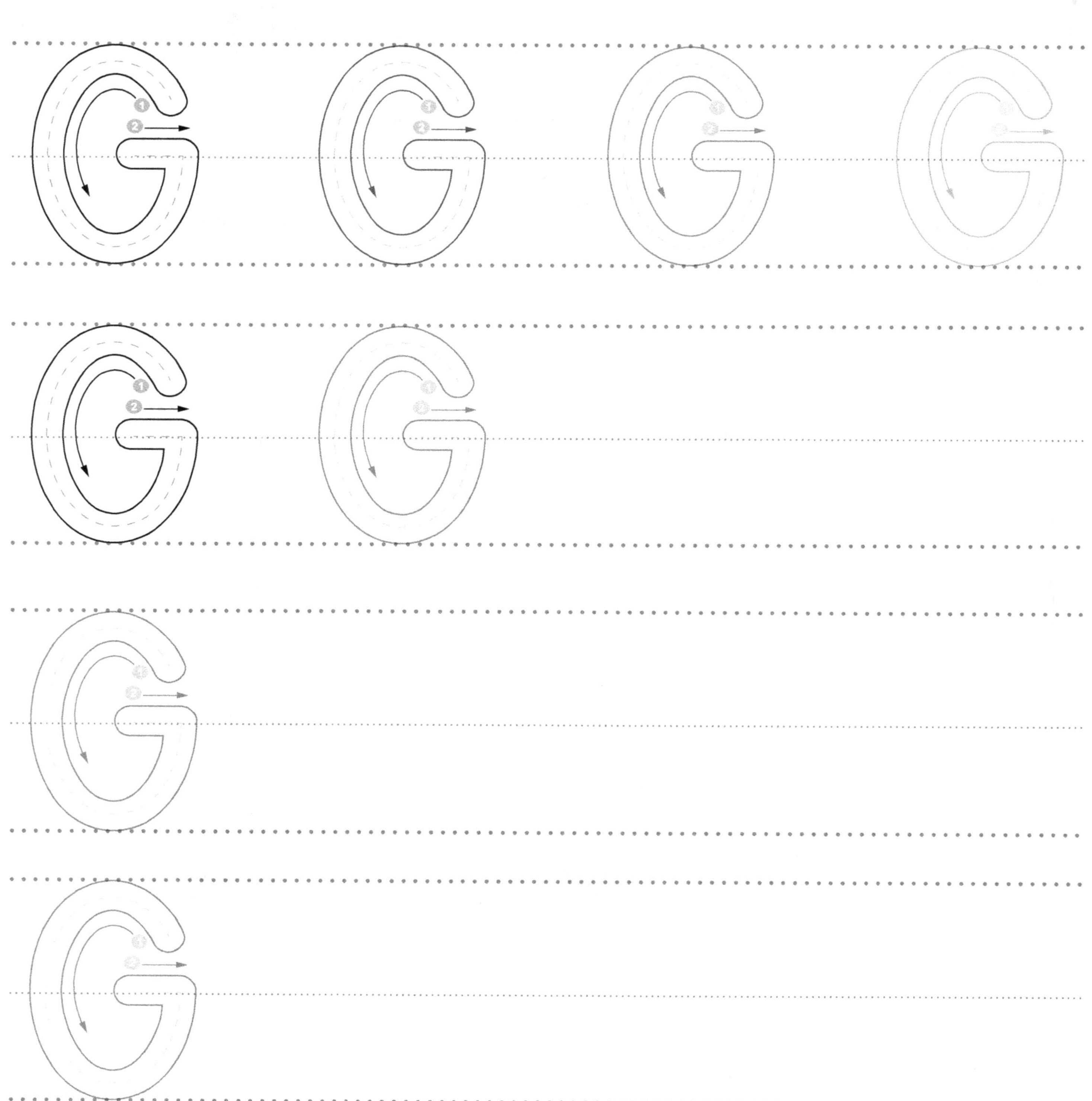

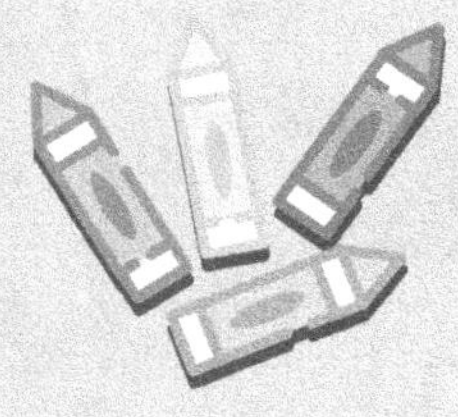

Find every G and color the sections

Cabbagedu

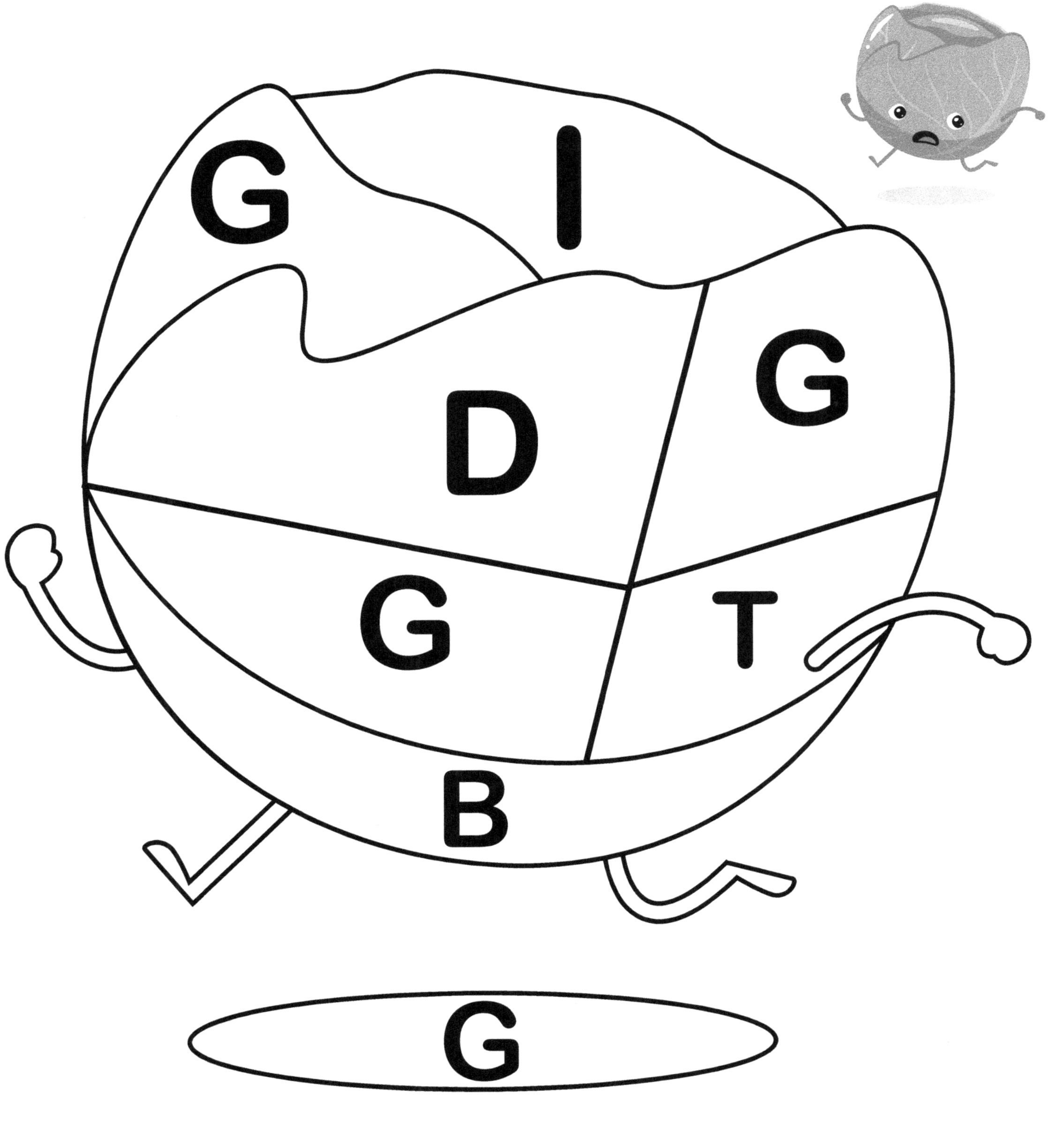

Find every g and circle them

g for goat

Trace the dotted line and read out loud

g for giraffe

Draw lines to match

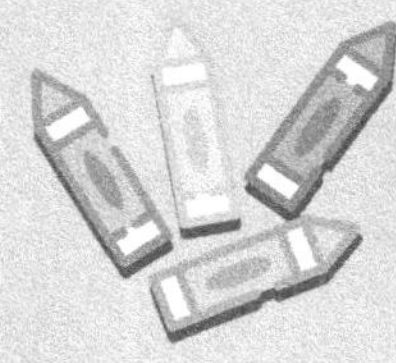

s
g
k
g
r
g
b
g
h
g

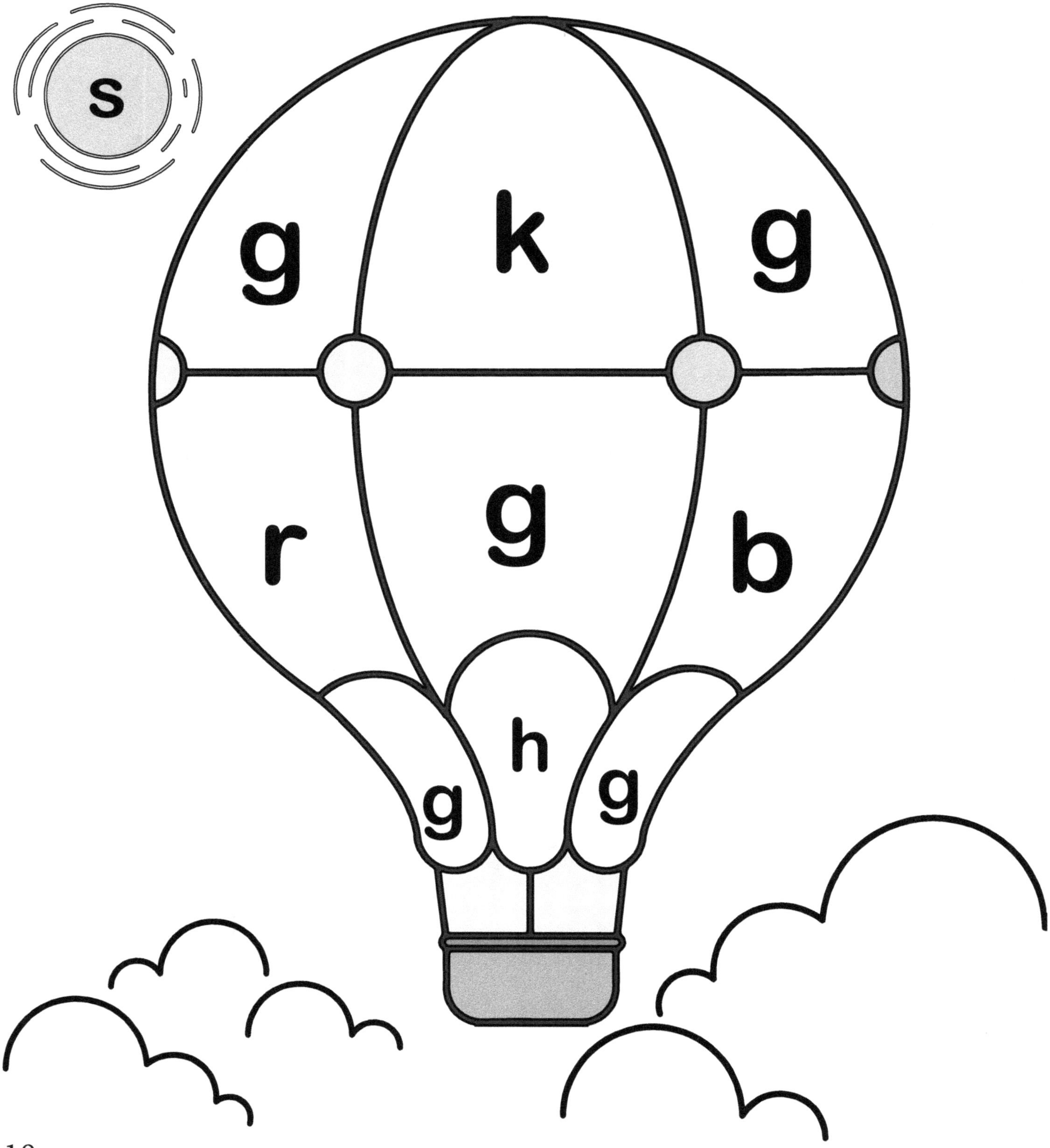

Trace the dotted line and read out loud

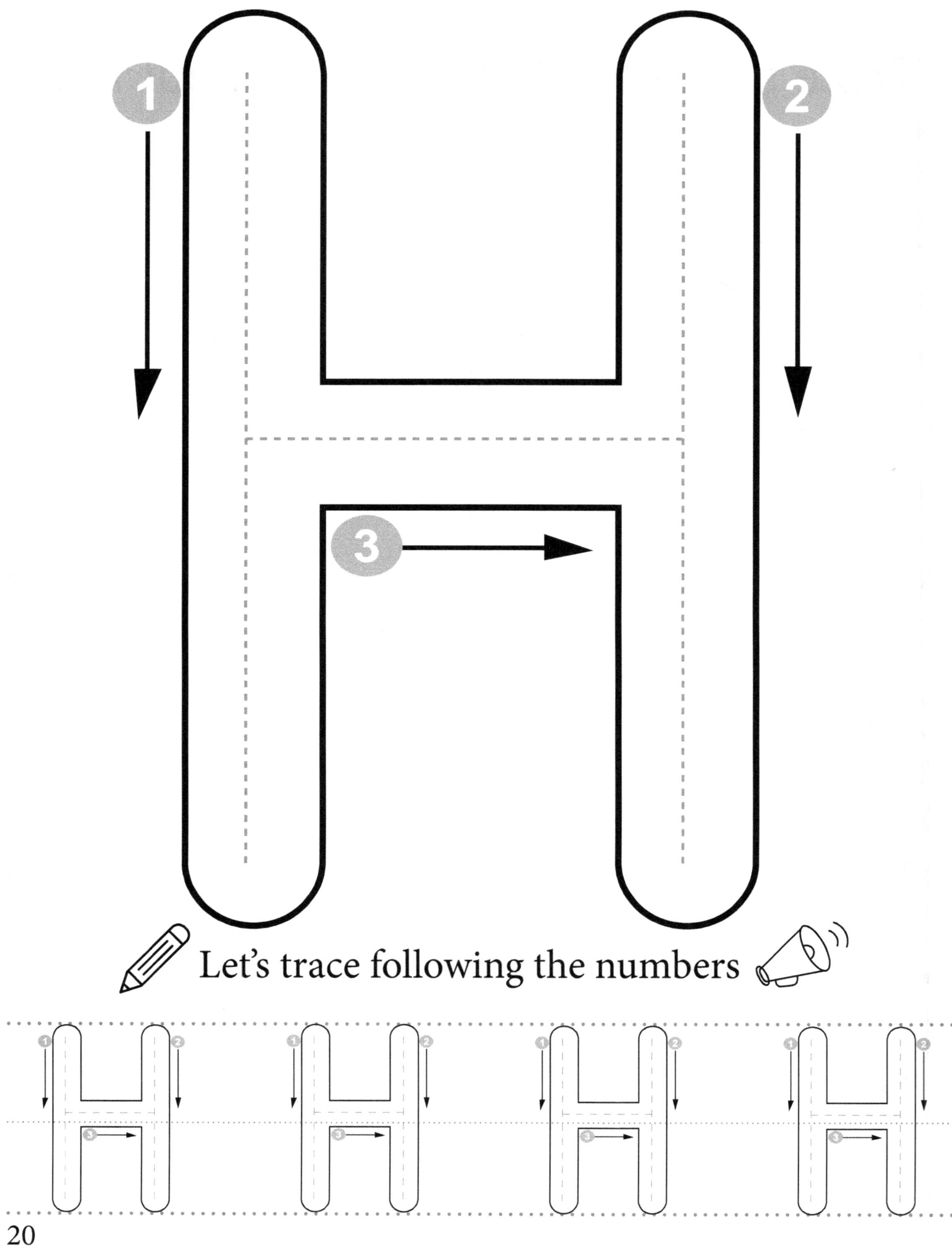

1
2
3
Let's trace following the numbers

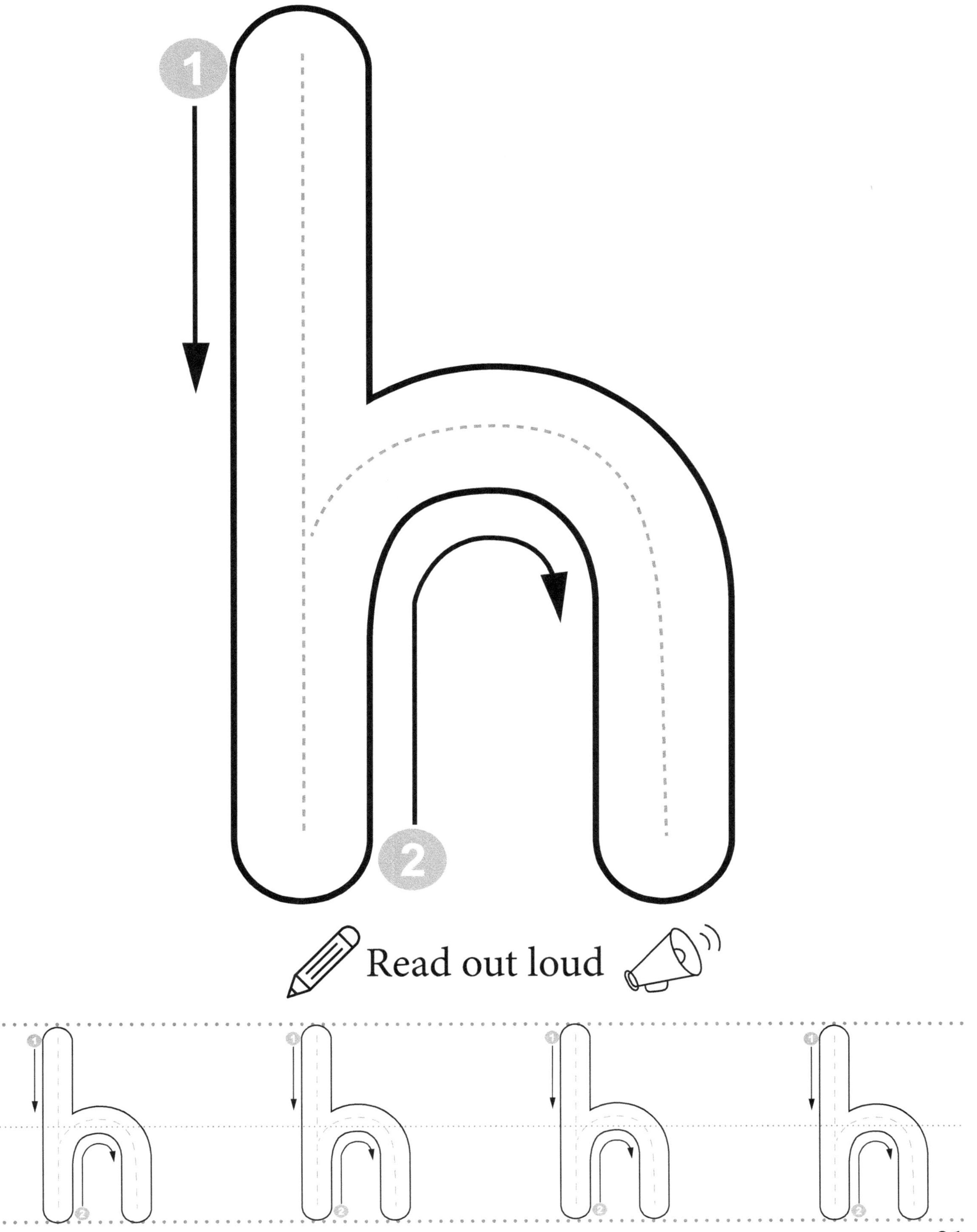

1
2
Read out loud

 Let's trace following the numbers 

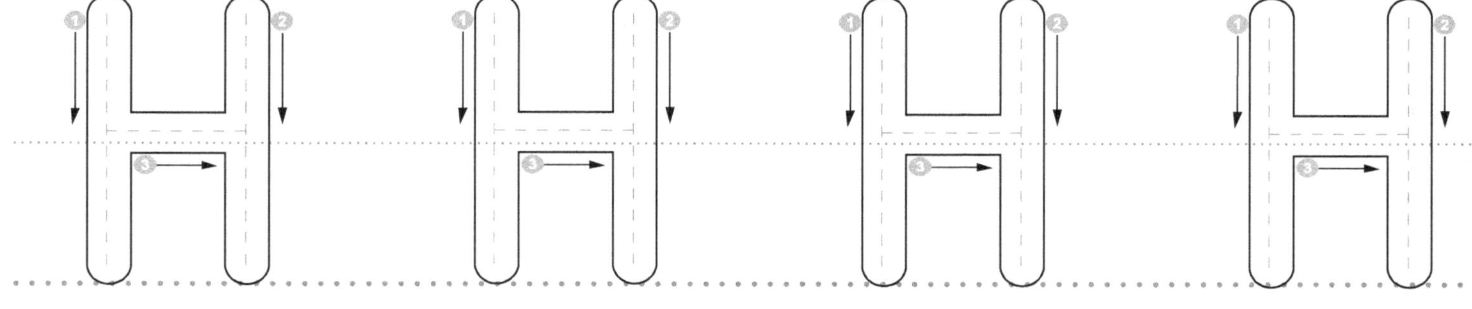

hat

h h h h

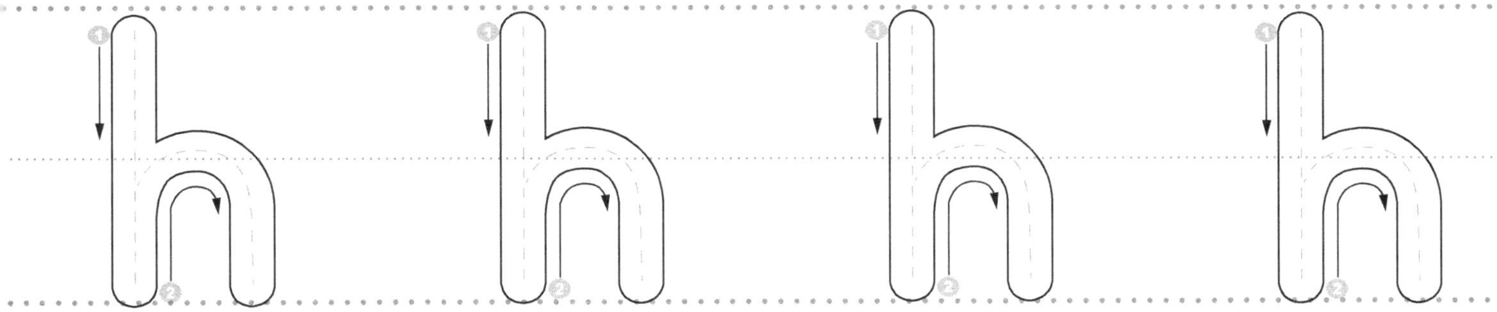

horse

Find every H and color them

S
H
H
O
X
J
H

You are doing
amazing!

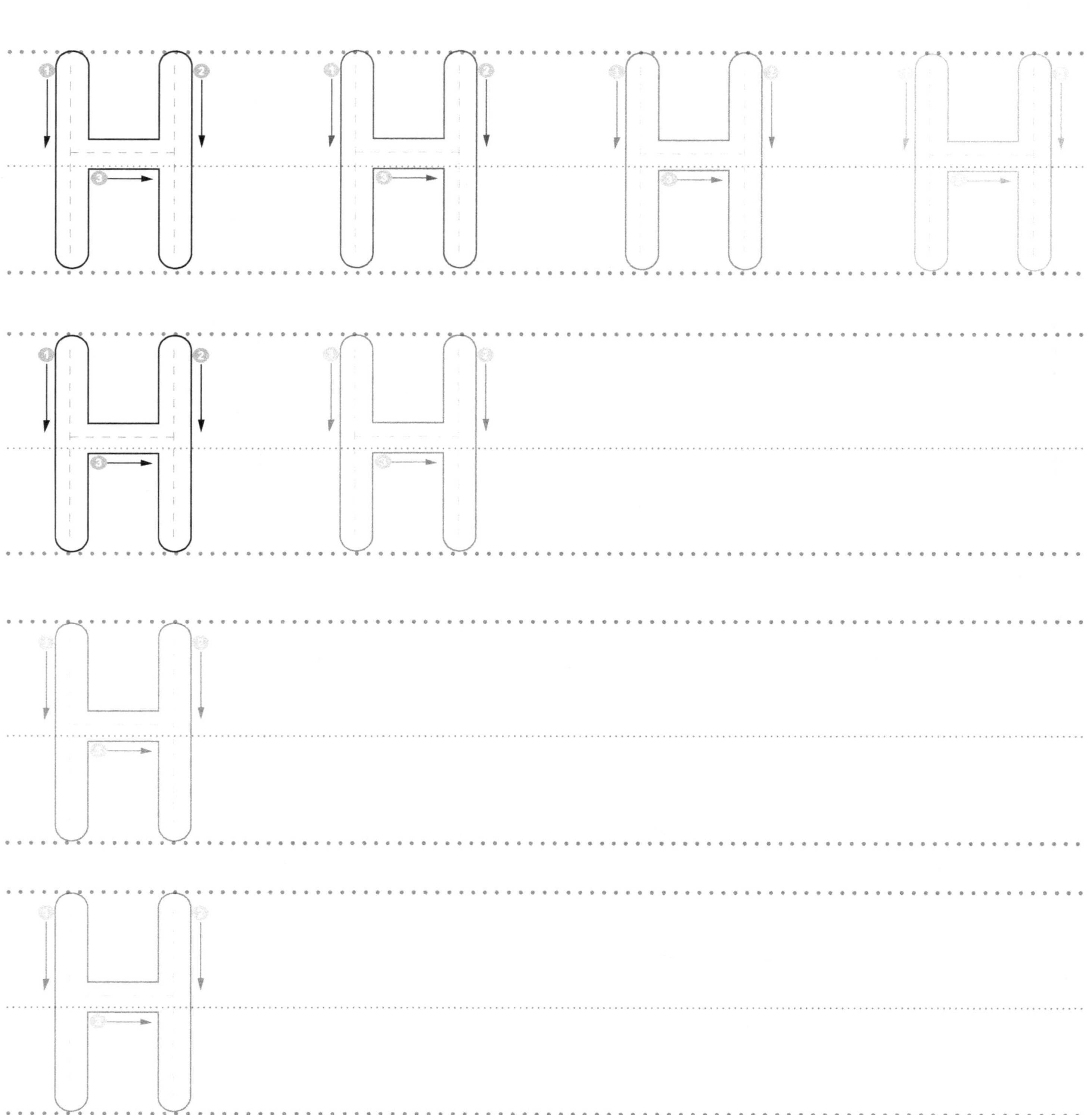

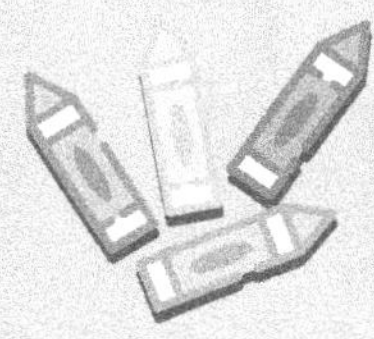

Find every H and color the sections

Cabbagedu

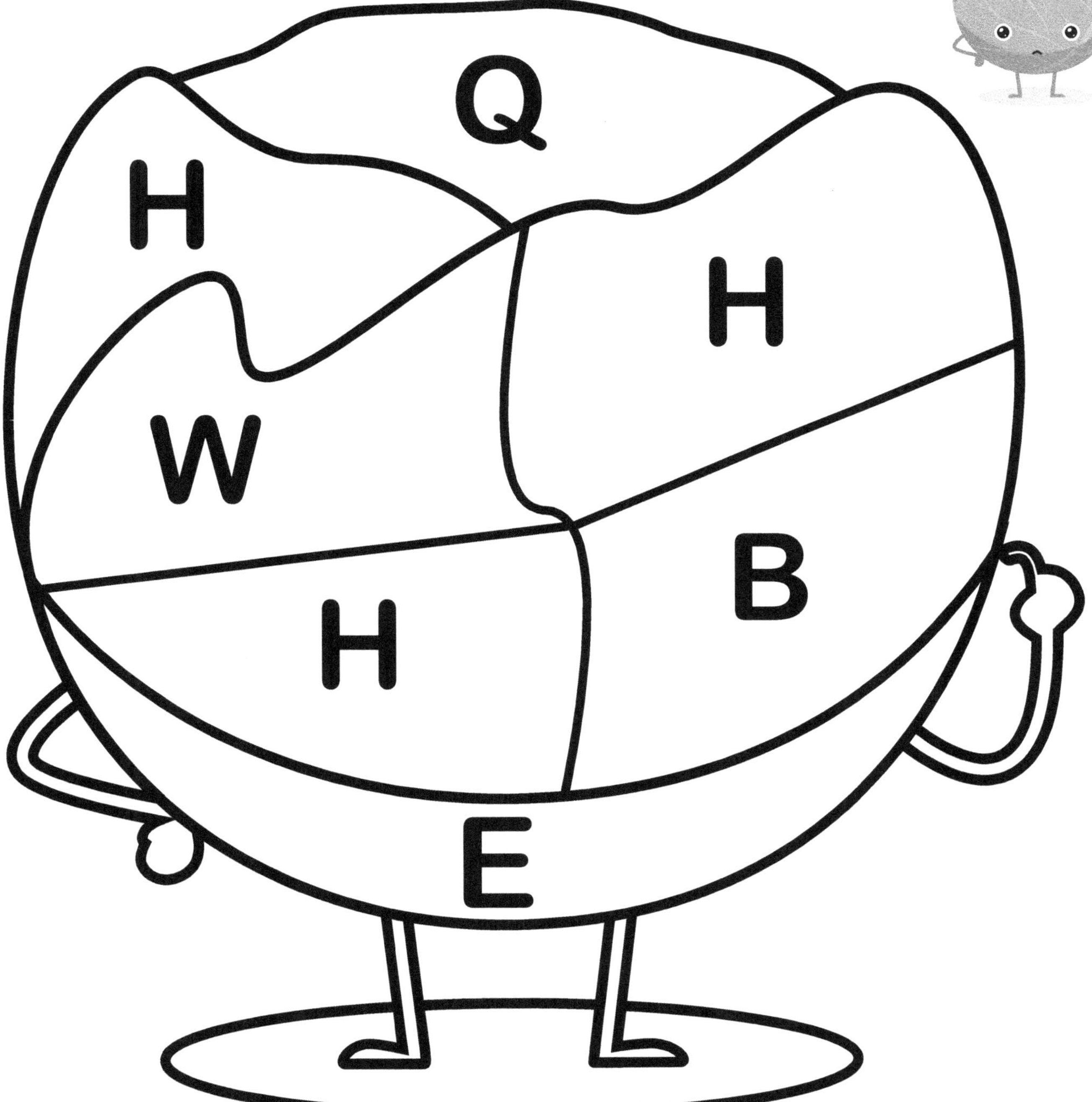

h for hat

Trace the dotted line and read out loud

Draw lines to match

h for horse

h
s
h
j
h
h
a
h
e
h

Trace the dotted line and read out loud

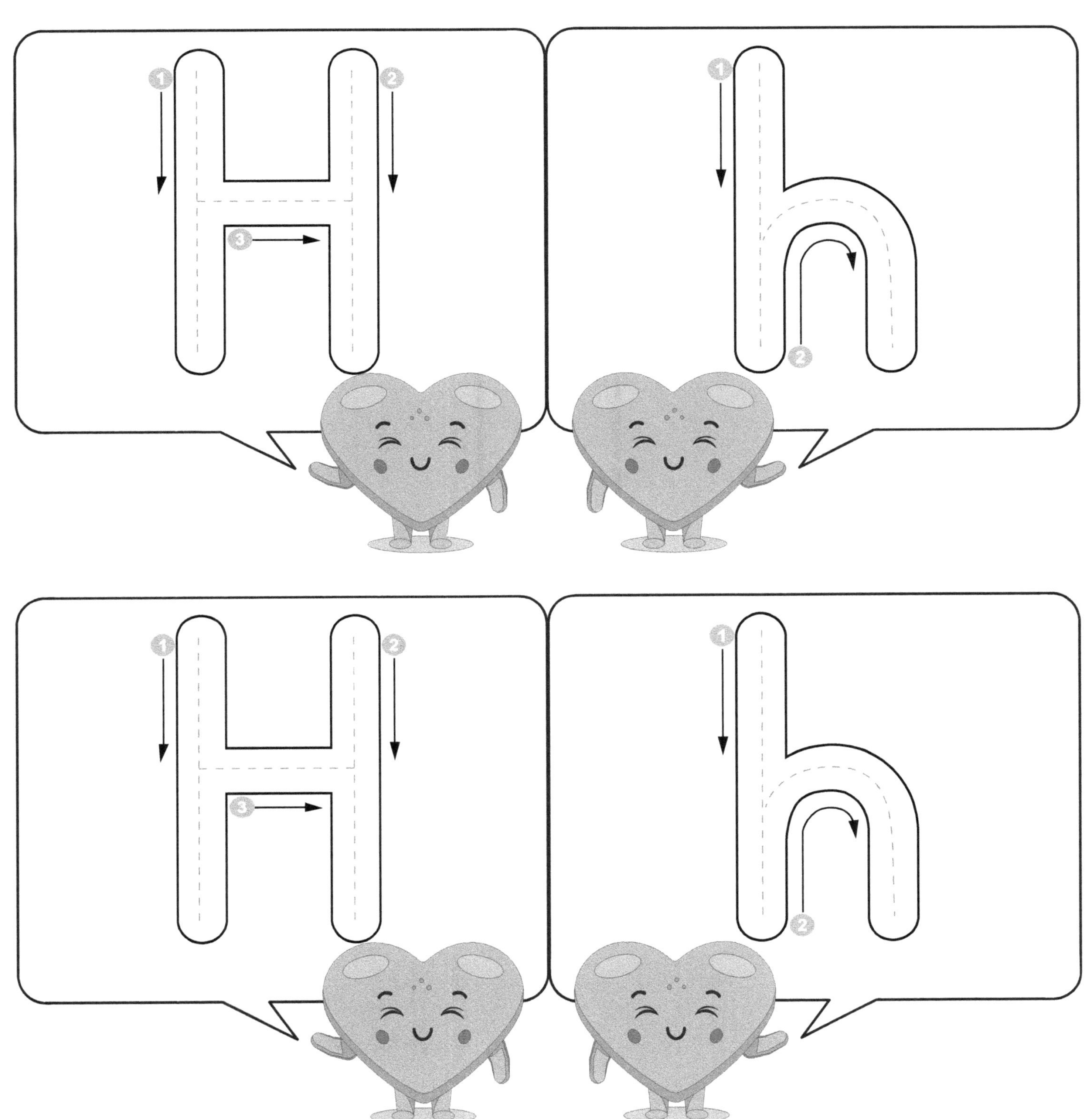

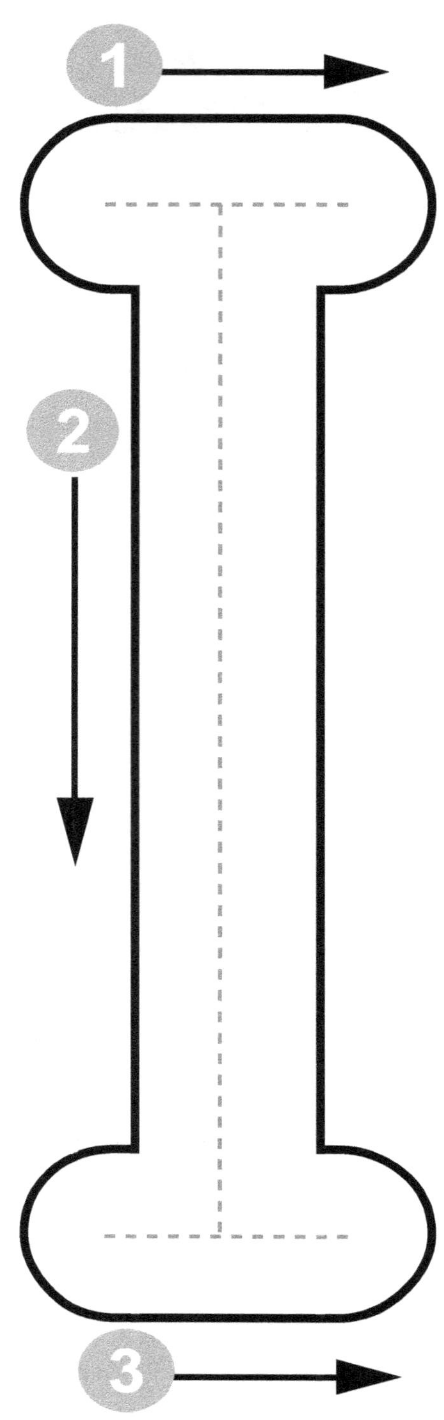

Let's trace following the numbers

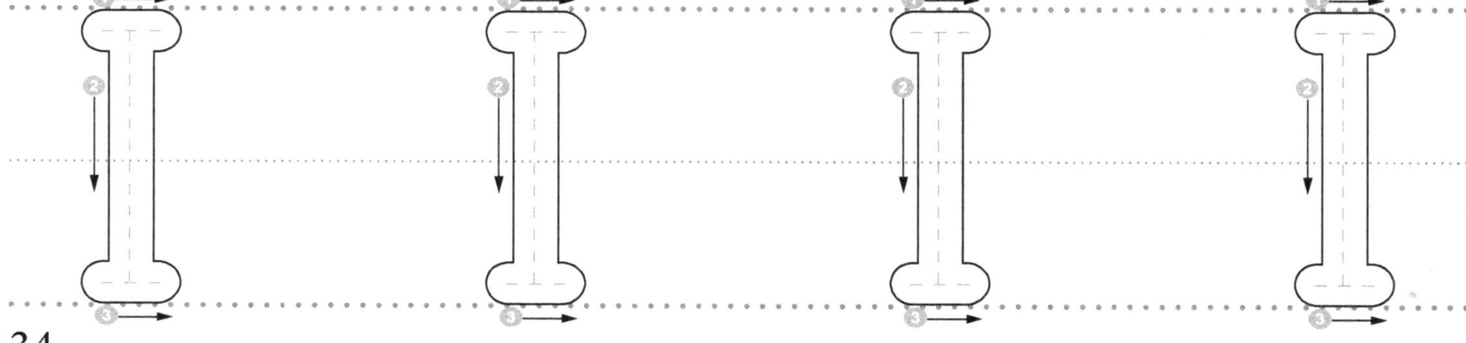

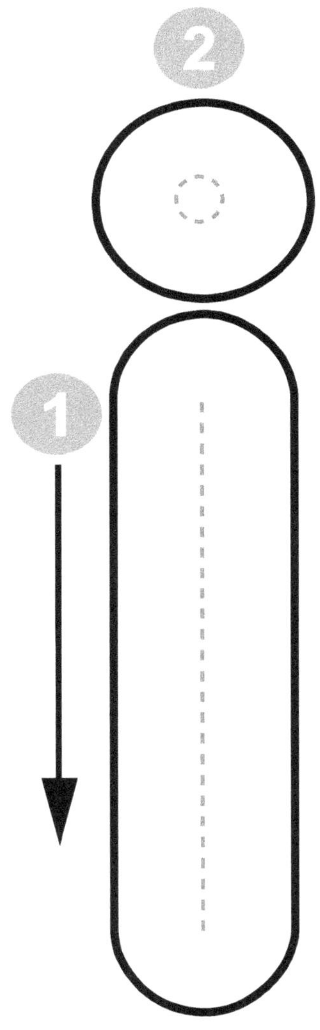

 Read out loud 

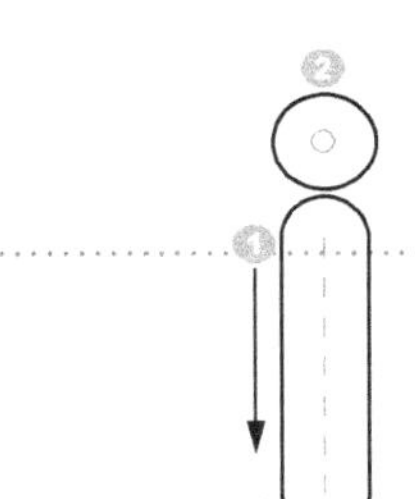 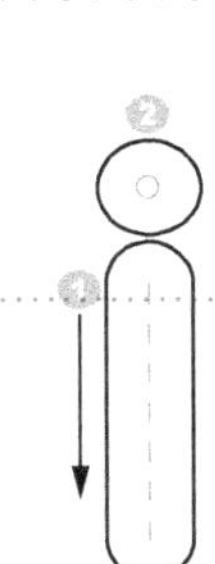 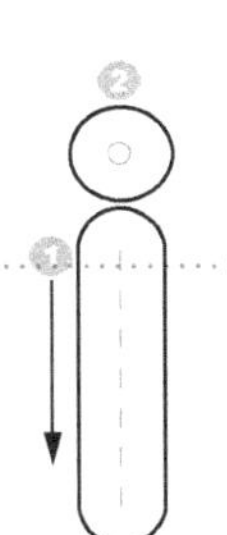 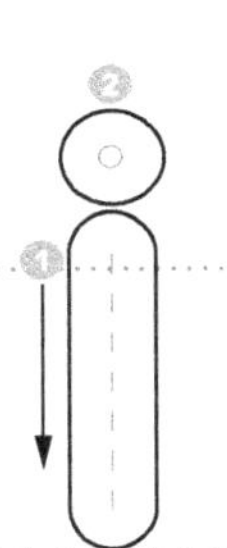

Ice cream

Let's trace following the numbers

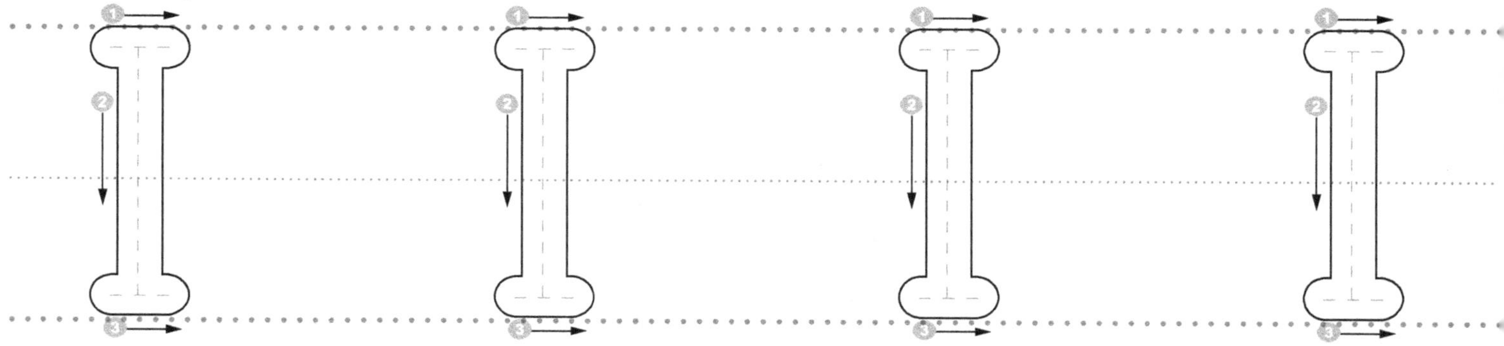

Island

ink

 Read out loud 

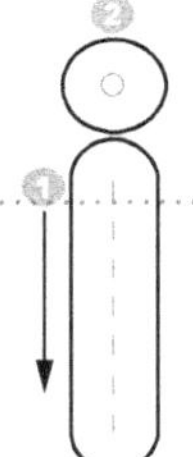 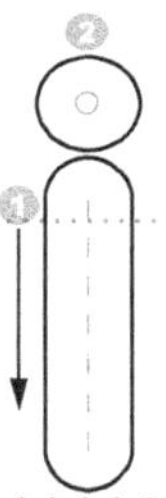 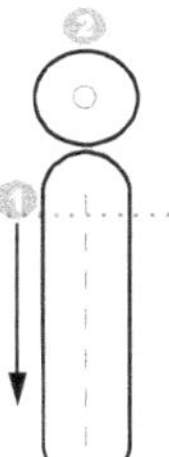 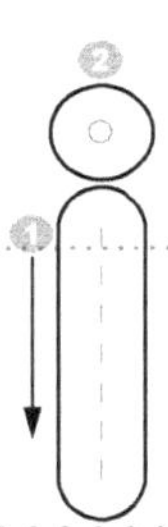

insect

I
P
I
X
P
F
F
I
Z
I

Well done!
I can see you're really trying!

Trace the dotted line and read out loud

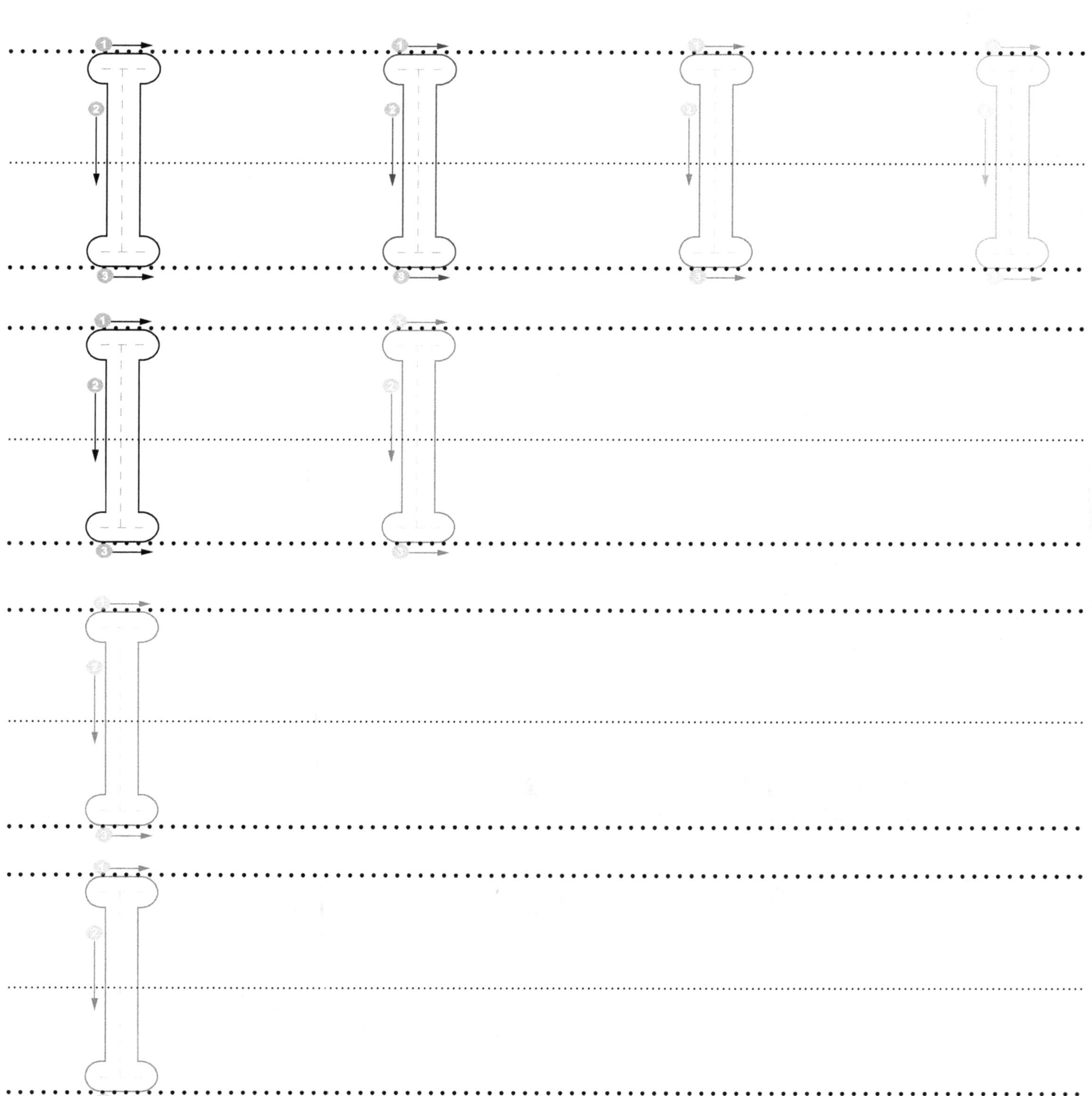

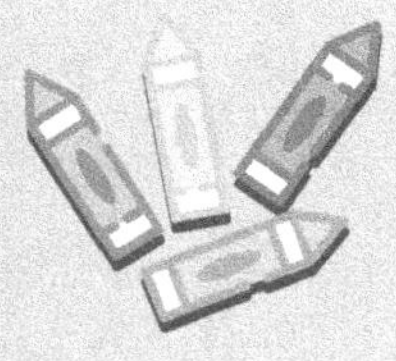

Find every I and color the sections

Cabbagedu

i for ice cream

Trace the dotted line and read out loud

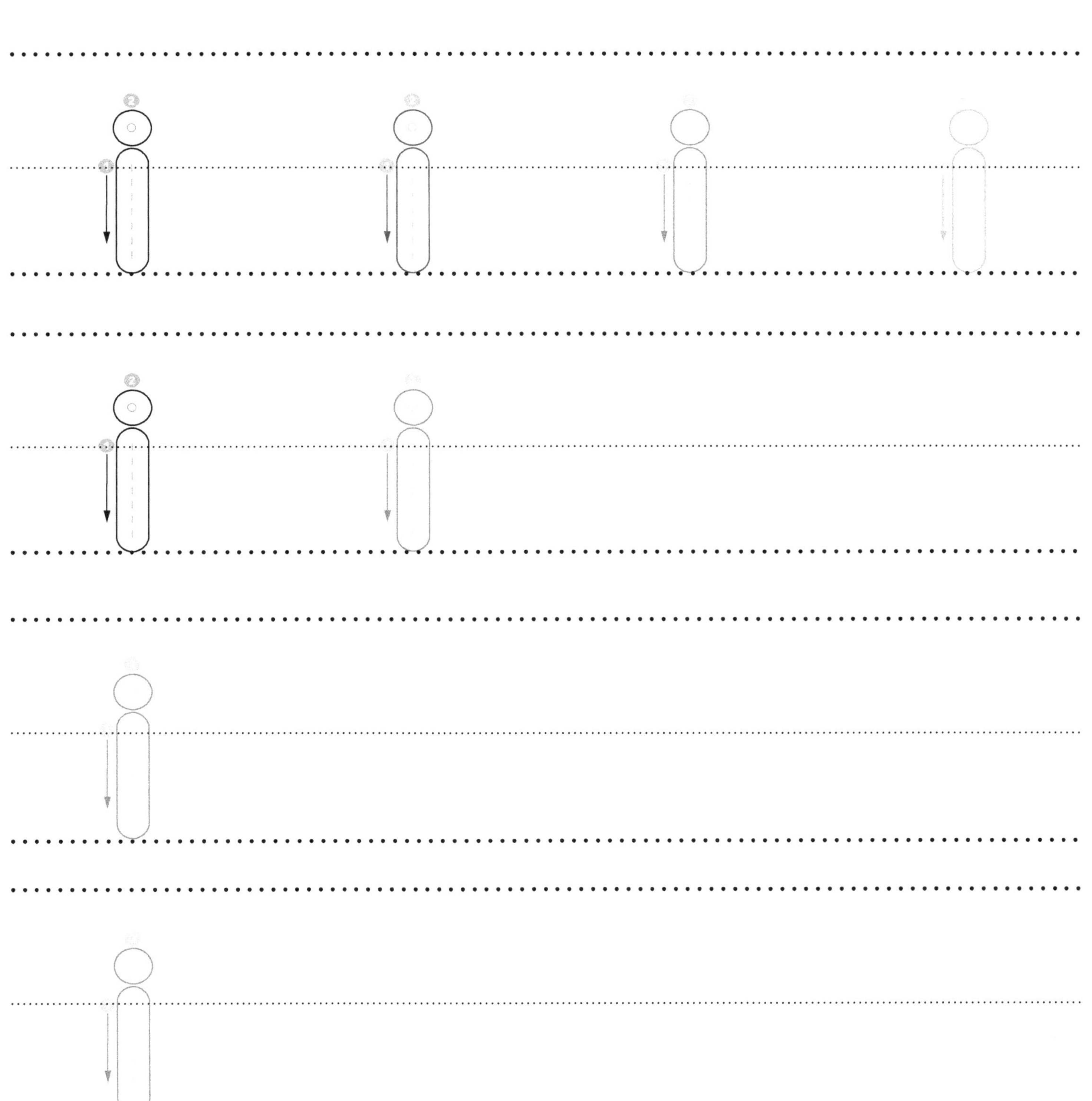

i for insect

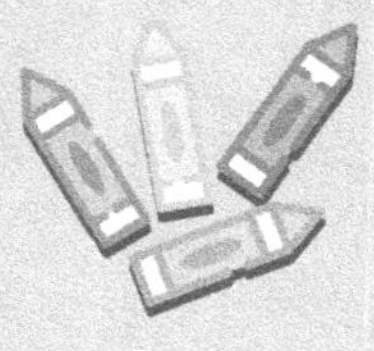

Find every i and color the sections

Trace the dotted line and read out loud

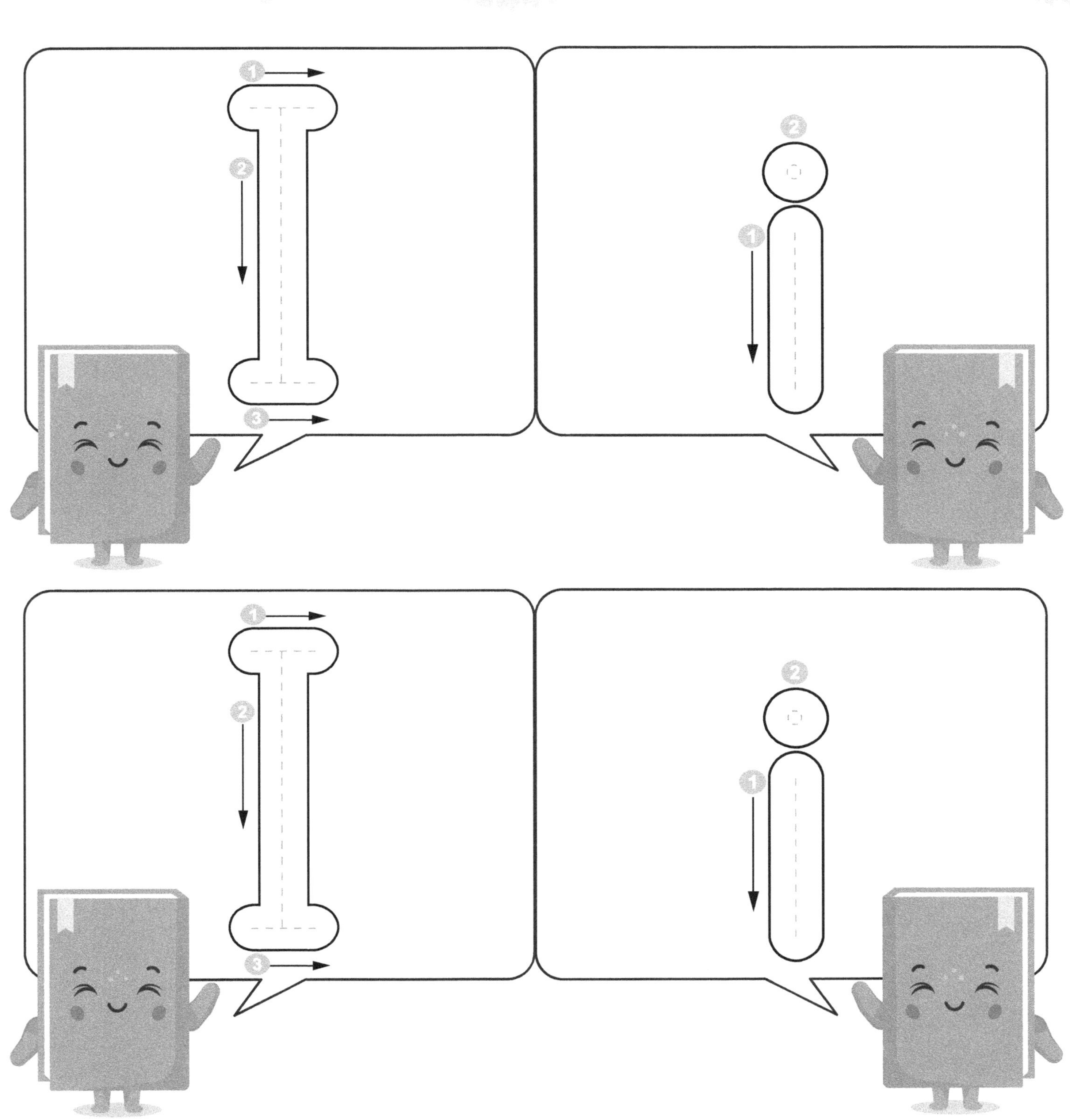

Where is Cabbagedu?

Find and circle!

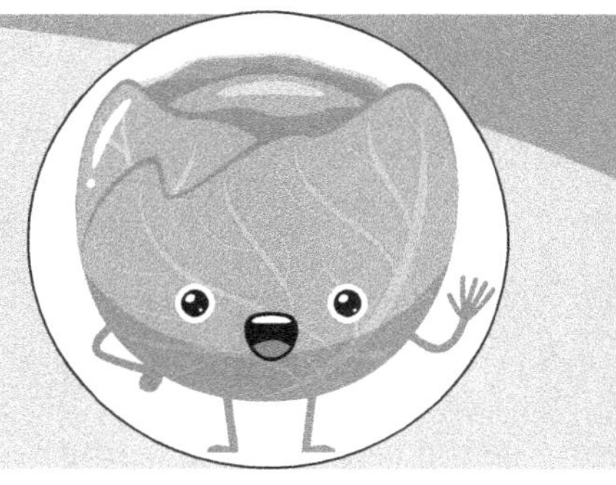

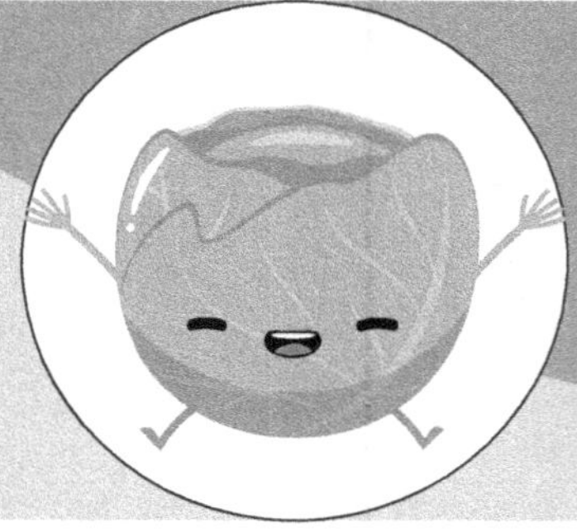

I am cool

I am hungry

I am playful

I am proud

I am okay

feelings with Cabbagedu!

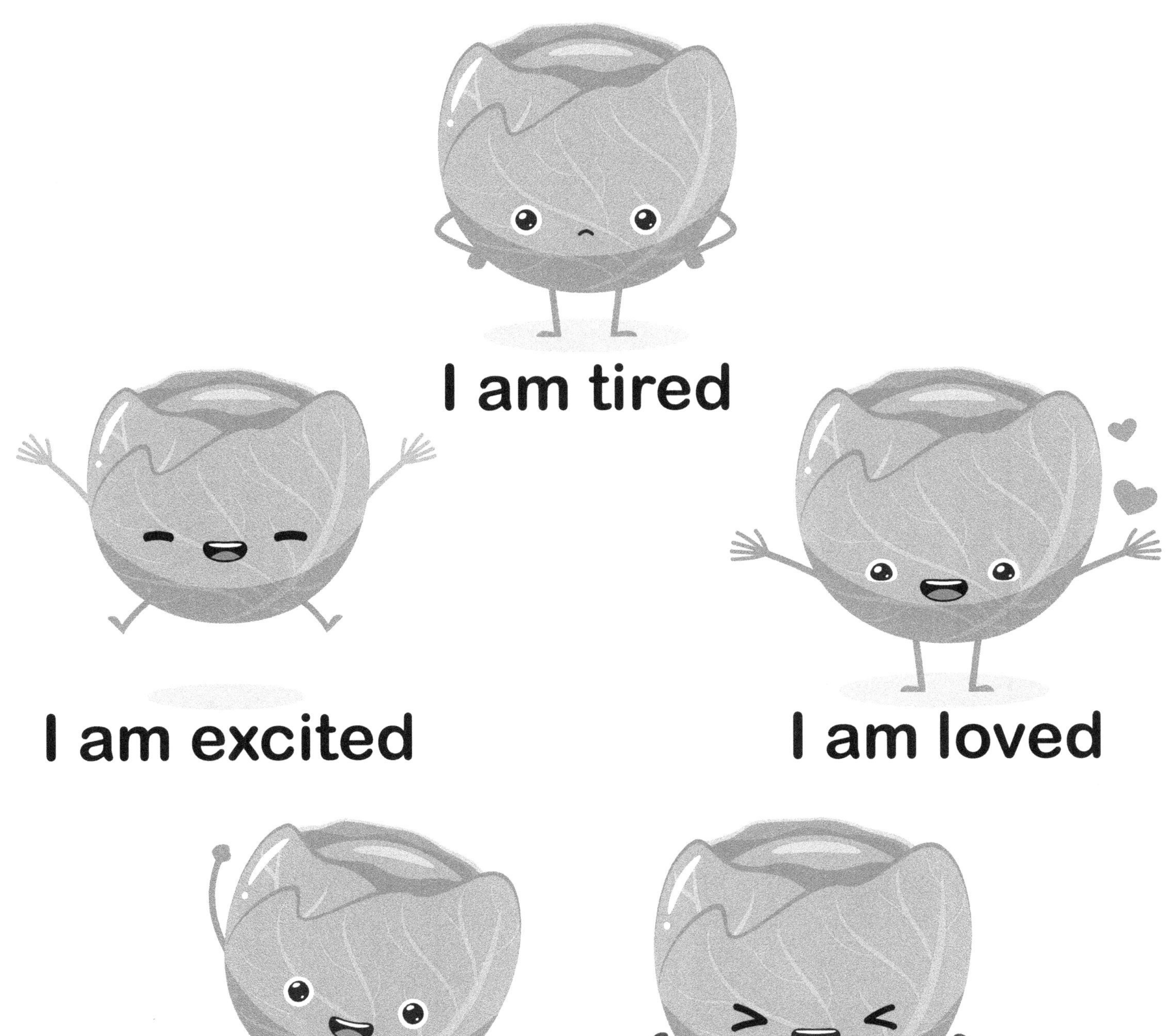

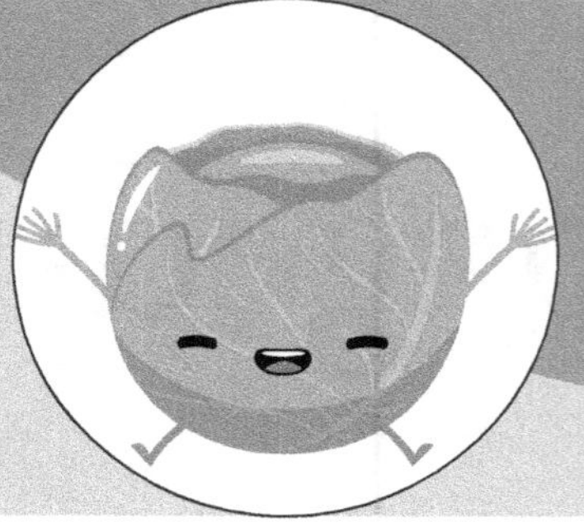

Let's express your

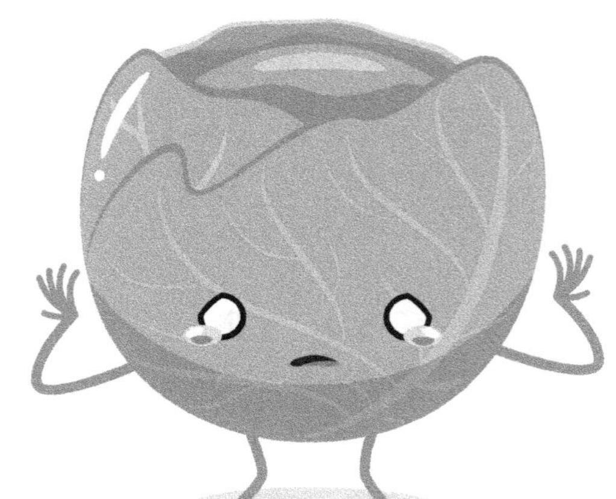

I am sad

I am calm

I am rushing

I am frustrated   I am angry

feelings with Cabbagedu!

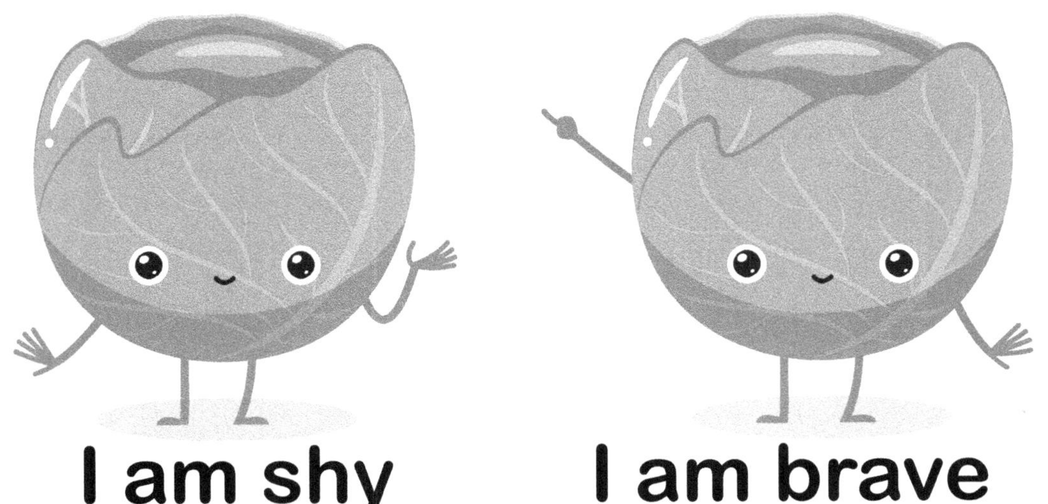

Write GHI and read out loud

Write ghi and read out loud

Awesome! We finished the book together!

Award

You are amazing!

This award is for

_______________   _______________
(first name)   (last name)

Great job finishing the book!

Date: _______________

Visit Our Website

BigSailorEdu.com

and Get Free & Fun

Educational Material

ABC Workbook Series by Big Sailor Edu

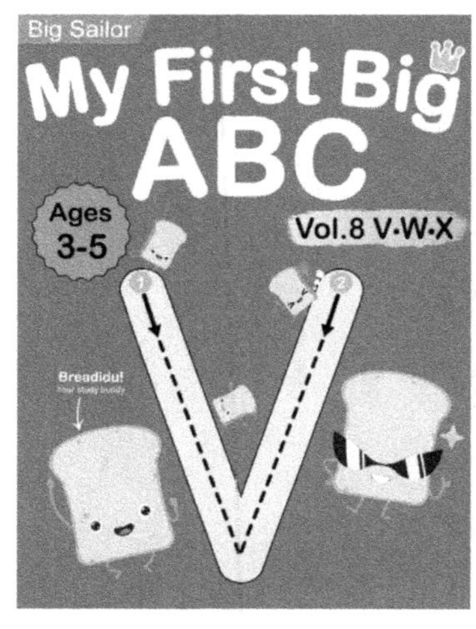

Cambridge Dynasty Press